COCCI
SHARDS

Lorenzo Chiera

C O C C I
(Frammenti di Versi)

traduzione di Lawrence Ferlinghetti
con la collaborazione di Massimiliano Chiamenti

For copyright information, see page 96

Lorenzo Chiera

SHARDS
(Fragments of Verses)

translation by Lawrence Ferlinghetti
in collaboration with Massimiliano Chiamenti

A NEW DIRECTIONS BOOK

Lorenzo Chiera (1348⁄1400?) nato al Testaccio, antico lembo di Roma famoso per il suo monte dei cocci, periferia paludosa della città imperiale nel Medioevo e anche da prima quando le navi di Tiro vi scaricavano i loro carichi di anfore (piene di olio e vino) dalle fornaci di tutto il Mediter⁄ raneo, Lorenzo Chiera certamente frequentava il quartiere attorno alla piramide di Caio Cestio adiacente la mura Aureliane vicino porta S. Pa⁄ olo e via Marmorata, piazza dell'Emporio e il ponte Sublicio.

Quasi niente può essere scoperto su di lui. Dev'essere stato per lo meno lettarato, un copista, forse uno stalliere, un ladruncolo, o un oste. E deve esser vissuto e morto senza che nessuno abbia mai registrato con precisione nascita e morte (ho congetturato le sue date da prove circostanziali frammentarie), e probabilmente non abbandonò il circondario di nascita, quel rozzo borghetto alla lontana ombra di Trastevere.

Quel poco che si è potuto scoprire della sua bassa esistenza proviene essenzialmente da fram⁄ menti di frasi (urli primigeni!) incise su sacchi di

Lorenzo Chiera (1348–1400?) born in Testaccio, ancient *lembo* of Rome famous for its *monte dei cocci* (hill of broken pottery), a swampy outskirt of the imperial city in the Middle Ages and before, when Tyrian ships unloaded their cargoes, amphorae (filled with oil and wine) from the kilns of all the Mediterranean, Lorenzo Chiera evidently frequented the quarter around the pyramid of Caio Cestio, close by the walls of Aurelius, near the Porta S. Paolo and the Via Marmorata, the Piazza dell'Emporio, and the Sublicio bridge.

Hardly anything can be discovered of him. He must have been at least literate, a scrivener by day, perhaps a hostler, a cut-purse, or a bar-keep. And he must have lived and died without anyone ever having exactly recorded his birth and death (I have conjectured his dates from fragmentary circumstantial evidence), and he probably never left the neighborhood of his birth, that rough borough in the far shadow of the Trastevere.

The little that anyone has been able to discover of his lowly existence comes mainly from fragments of phrases (primeval cries!) scratched on

tela o piccoli pezzi di pergamena grezza o carta da macellaio (questi ultimi forse essendo numerosi al Testaccio, non molto distanti da dove i grandi macelli della città nutrivano di sangue il Tevere, imporporandone le acque), abbozzate da lui stesso o da qualcuno che lo sentiva parlare o cantare in stato di ubriachezza in qualche ritrovo plebeo.

Che Chiera probabilmente morisse in una rissa di taverna fa pensare a quel giovane genio violento che fu Christopher Marlow, il quale andò incontro a Londra ad una fine analoga in un secolo leggermente posteriore. Ad ogni modo, sia le prove interne che quelle esterne sono tenui, come d'altronde tutto ciò che riguarda l'identità di Chiera e le sue origini, essendo un puzzle il suo stesso nome, che porta sia la radice del congiuntivo di "desidero" in spagnolo (che suo padre fosse giunto su una nave mercantile dalla Spagna o dal Portogallo?), ma anche suonando in italiano come "Chi era?"...

Sebbene chi fosse Chiera rimarrà probabilmente un mistero, i frammenti dei suoi versi orali che sono in qualche modo giunti fino a noi tramite

fiber sacks or thin scraps of crude parchment or butcher 'paper' (the latter perhaps being plentiful in the Testaccio not very far from where the city's great slaughterhouses fed blood to the Tiber, incarnadining the waters), scrawled by himself or someone who heard him speak or sing drunkenly in some low retreat.

That Chiera perhaps died in a tavern brawl makes one think of that young violent genius Christopher Marlowe in London who suffered a similar death in a slightly later century. However, the external and internal evidence is slight, as is everything having to do with Chiera's identity and origins, his very name being a puzzle, bearing the subjunctive roots of "I wish" in Spanish (did his father arrive by trading ship from Spain or Portugal?) but also in Italian sounding like "Who was" (Chi era?) ...

Even though "who was" Chiera will probably always remain a mystery, the scraps of his voiceverse that have somehow descended to us through rough unknown hands attest to a libidinous spirit

rozze mani sconosciute testimoniano di uno spirito libidinoso che si erge dal bagliore cupo del tardo Medioevo europeo (come il primo bagliore di luce nelle tele prerinascimentali – vividamente evocato da Ruskin nella sua storia della pittura così ossessionata dalla luce). È la luce dello sperma, umano o animale.

E davvero è quasi come se Chiera fosse uno di quegli avidi esseri androgini dei dipinti orgiastici di Hieronymus Bosch che a sua volta sembrava proprio essere appena sopravissuto ai Secoli Bui.

Udento Chiero per la prima volta, ci si rende subito conto che siamo in presenza di una selvaggia coscienza erotica, come se i sensi guidati dal desiderio si fossero improvvisamente svegliati da un sonno ativico di mille anni, una giovinezza svegliata da una rozza mano medievale, i sensi ancora in fremito, ubriaca nella stiva di una qualche nave da schiavi, non in grado di distinguere la notte dal giorno né la vista dall'udito, con l'occhio, l'orecchio ed il naso che si confondono l'uno

rising out of the damp gloom of Europa's late dark ages (like the first glimmer of light in pre-renaissance canvasses — as so vividly evoked by Ruskin in his light-obsessed history of painting). It is the light of sperm, human or animal.

And indeed it is almost as if Chiera were one of those androgynous beings in the orgiastic paintings of Hieronymus Bosch who also seemed just to have escaped the dark ages.

Hearing Chiera for the first time, we soon realize we are in the presence of a savage erotic consciousness, as if the lust-driven senses were suddenly awakened out of a hoary sleep of a thousand years, a youth shaken awake by a rude medieval hand, senses still reeling, drunk in the hold of some slave ship, not knowing night from day nor sight from sound, the eye and the ear and the nose confounding each other, not yet knowing which function each was to take up in the quivering dawn.

I here set down best as I can (knowing little

con l'altro, senza sapere quale funzione doveva assumere ciascuno nell'alba palpitante.

Ho qui steso meglio che ho potuto (conoscendo poco del Romaesco antico e ancor meno del demoniaco Latino) tutto ciò che sono riuscito a decifrare e a rendere coerente delle tracce frammentate della sua voce, che immagino sia stata una voce profonda, e tuttavia con la sveglia sensibilità da furbo mozzo che si affida alle percezioni fisiche e alle intuizioni per sopravvivere in un mondo per il quale non è adeguato.

È volgare. È matto. È incivile. Tuttavia è innocente. "Sempre più truffate, le folle rincorrono specchietti per le allodole" (William Burroughs). Ma il rozzo innocente sopravvive nel suo proprio mondo, mentre altri trascrivono i suoi suoni primigeni su fogli di pergamena . . .

LAWRENCE FERLINGHETTI

of early Romanesco or Roman dialects nor less demonic Latin) all that I can decipher and make coherent from the broken traces of his voice, which I imagine to have been a deep voice yet with the alert *furbo* sensitivity of a roustabout who relies on physical perceptions and intuition to survive in a world he's not dressed for.

He's vulgar. He's mad. He's uncouth. Yet he is innocent. "Swept with con the millions stand under the signs" (William Burroughs). But the rough innocent survives in his own world, as others write down his primal sounds on parchment leaves ...

LAWRENCE FERLINGHETTI

Cocci

[...]

Rossegnetto[1] capa[2] a chançona chantare
sopre[3] lo loto[4] de casolare

[...]

Ène[5] Tiestaccio lo meo mustaccio
donne[6] callo[7] laite[8] de vita prochaccio

[...]

1   Rossegnetto: 'usignuolo'.
2   Capa: 'scegli'.
3   Sopre: 'sopra'.
4   Loto: 'fango'.
5   Ène: 'è'.
6   Donne: 'da cui'.
7   Callo: 'caldo'.
8   Laite: 'latte'.

Shards

*

Think what song to sing
on the roof of this
mud hovel
little nightingale

*

Testaccio
my moustachio
through which I suck
life's hot milk

*

[...]

La nebbia scenne[9] sopre Tristevere
[iacese[10]] onne veone[11]
ne le soa viçione[12] [...]

[...]

9   Scenne: 'scende'.
10   Iacese: 'si giace'.
11   Veone: 'beone'.
12   Ne le soa viçione: 'nei suoi vaneggiamenti'.

*

And heavy hangs the fog
from Trastevere
where every drunken sod
[lies] lost in revery

*

[…]

Joie o trestitia […]
lucono lucora[13] sopre li ponne[14]
belle iente[15] que[16] vaco[17]
aitri a balle[18] […]
et battito de ale[19]
ne l'aere nigro[20]

[…]

13 Lucora: 'luci'.
14 Ponne: 'ponti'.
15 Iente: 'gente'.
16 Que: 'che'.
17 Vaco: 'vanno'.
18 Aitri a balle: 'altri (sottint. scendono) a valle'.
19 Ale: 'ali'.
20 Aere nigro: 'aria nera'.

*

Joy or misery ...
Lights at night on bridges
Figures passing fair
Others falling there
And beat of wings
in the black air

*

[…]

Et cossí no fusse[21] que la luce […]
resvigliato[22] et abafato[23] […]
como[24] fé[25] a l'alba allotta[26]
dericta ionse[27] de quella potta[28]

[…]

21   Fusse: 'fosse'.
22   Resvigliato: 'svegliato'.
23   Abafato: 'a bocca aperta'.
24   Como: 'come'.
25   Fé: 'fece'.
26   Allotta: 'allora'.
27   Dericta ionse: 'diritta giunse'.
28   Potta: 'vagina'.

*

So be it
Never again
will light ever
shake me awake
as it did that dawning
straight from the cunt
astounded

*

[...]

Appoiato[29] sopre lo capo meo tonno[30]
malaurato[31] celletto d'amore
canta lo canto sio[32] tristo
a l'auricla[33] mea dura [...]

[...]

29   Appoiato: 'appollaiato'.
30   Tonno: 'tondo'.
31   Malaurato: 'malaugurato'.
32   Sio: 'suo'.
33   Auricla: 'orecchio'.

*

Perched on my fat head
that fucking bird of love
sings sad songs
in my bad ear

*

[...]

Novamente la luna descenne[34]
como en ymago de bolon[gnino] culo[35]
drama d'ariento[36] [...]
anchora plena[37] de luce
que ne furao[38] [...]
ab la scuritate nuostra[39]

[...]

34 Descenne: 'scende'.
35 Como en ymago de bolon[gnino] culo: 'come in
    immagine di un culo a forma di monetina'.
36 Dramma d'ariento: 'dracma d'argento'.
37 Plena: 'piena'.
38 Ne furao: 'ci rubò'.
39 Ab la scuritate nuostra: 'dalla nostra oscurità'.

*

Down goes that moon again
that bare⁄ass coin
silver drachma
still full of the light
it stole from us
out of our darkness

*

[...]

Breareo[40] sul tetto
aguçço[41] monstro [...]
de contennere[42] a lo cielo hao[43] dilletto

[...]

---

40   Breareo: 'gigante'.
41   Aguçço: 'acuminato'.
42   Contennere: 'contendere'.
43   Hao: 'ha'.

*

Gargantua
on a rooftop
monster gothic tower
fucks old sky

*

[...]

Coccia[44] terra et ossa desfatte
zuccha de capore abafate[45]
auicla que alba ode,
ochio ch'ennasa[46] lo fummo
ode la squilla de fierro de lo champanile
que clama[47] de Paradiso
o de 'Nferno
sona lo meo tin∕tin
sona lo meo tin∕tin
tin∕tin campanin

[...]

44   Coccia: 'cocci', 'ossa'.
45   Zuccha de capore abafate: 'teschi a fauci aperte'.
46   Ennasa: 'annusa'.
47   Clama: 'chiama'.

*

Cocci clay bones broke
Skull agape
Ear feels dawn
Eye smells smoke
hears the iron steeple bell
call from heaven
or from hell
Pull my ding-dong
Pull my ding-dong
ding-dong bell

*

[…]

Quilli varvari[48] de Chrestiani
siempre amme dereto[49]
pe'ffacere me como illoro […]
ne lo miraglio[50] mirome
et veggio lo rebellante
donne siempre me cansettero[51]

[…]

48 Quilli varvari: 'quei barbari'.
49 Dereto: 'dietro'.
50 Miraglio: 'specchio'.
51 Me cansettero: 'mi tennero alla larga'.

*

Those barbarians
(the Christians)
still after me
to be like them
to be like them
I look in the glass
and see the lout
they always warned me about

*

[...]

Chiove[52] lo cielo sanguine
però ca[53] n'hao baratta[54]
reiaco[55] li sorci
i' configome[56]
ne lo meo amore

[...]

52 Chive: 'piove'.
53 Ca: 'che'.
54 N'hao baratta: 'c'è la guerra'.
55 Reiaco: 'regnano'.
56 Confugome: 'mi rifugio'.

*

Sky rains blood
It's war
Rats take over
I take cover
In my lover

*

[...]

Isfacciata sora
vestuta[57] de vestora[58] de ballacchino[59]
dereto lo velame [...]
u' colase[60] la Vergene [...]
mettiveme la lengua ne la vocca[61]
essenno guarzone de decimoquarto[62]
et [...] polluere[63] [...]

[...]

57 Vestuta: 'vestita'.
58 Vestora: 'vesti'.
59 Ballacchino: 'seta'.
60 U' colase: 'dove si venera'.
61 Vocca: 'bocca'.
62 Essenno guarzone de decimoquarto: 'quando ero un
    ragazzino di quattordici anni'.
63 Polluere (latino): 'eiaculare'.

*

Sexy Nonny
in her silk nun's habit
behind the arras
of the cult of the Virgin
stuck her tongue in my mouth
when I was fourteen

Made me cream

*

[...]

Dereto a lo maciello trescharremo[64]
però ca dereto lo pellagetto[65]
destesi ne l'herba
como li cani farremo

[...]

---

64   Trescharremo: 'balleremo'.
65   Pellagetto: 'piccolo stagno, deposito di acqua'.

*

Shall we dance?
Behind the slaughterhouse
up behind the reservoir
stretched in the long grasses
we'll do it like dogs

*

[…]

Co le zinne tra le mee gamme[66]
cossì fé […]
I' colava[67] la capa[68] soa
ella lo ne manichava[69]
mugolanno[70]

[…]

66   Gamme: 'gambe'.
67   Colava: 'cullavo'.
68   Capa: 'testa'.
69   Lo ne manichava: 'ce lo mangiava'.
70   Mugolanno: 'mugolando'.

*

Breasts between my legs
she did it to me
I her head cradled
as it ate me
moaning

*

[…]

Callo[71] lo sole
calla[72] la soa offella[73] de amore
calla la palommella[74]
ca de aito descenneva[75]

[…]

71 Callo: 'caldo'.
72 Calla: 'calda'.
73 Offella: 'focaccia'.
74 Palommella: 'colombella'.
75 Ca de aito descenneva: 'che discendeva dall'alto'.

*

Hot the sun

Hot her bun of love

Hot the dove descending

from above

*

[…]

Futteime[76] propio[77] como le fere[78]
et como amarme potuera[79]
et i' ad illui sanz'esto facere[80]?

[…]

76 Futteime: 'mi fotté'.
77 Propio: 'proprio'.
78 Fere: 'bestie'.
79 Potuera: 'potrebbe'.
80 Sanz'esto facere: 'senza fare questo'.

*

On all fours
he buggered me
How could he
love me
without doing it
(And I he)
?

*

[...]

Ah pure la dama genzora[81]
se revoltola[82] ne l'herba
no simo forze[83] tutti animale[84]
Quattro iambe per amare
embreccecati[85] uno torno de l'aitro[86]
empeciati enzieme[87]
nel vespero

[...]

81   Genzora: 'più elegante'.
82   Revoltola: 'rotola'.
83   No simo forze: 'non siamo forse'.
84   Animale: 'animali'.
85   Embreccecati: 'abbracciati'.
86   Aitro: 'alto'.
87   Empeciati enzieme: 'appiccicati insieme'.

*

Ah that high lady too
rolls in the hay
Are we not all animals
Four legs to love with
Wound around each other
stuck together
in the dusk

*

[. . .]

De vanitate addorna
esta facultosa femina
de latere spurgao[88]
como habaria[89] cornato[90] nu villano
et no vulessine gustarne

[. . .]

<hr>

88 De latere spurgao: 'sputò da una parte'.
89 Habaria: 'avesse'.
90 Cornato: 'succhiato (per *fellatio*)'.

*

Full of fancy airs
this rich bitch
just spit to the side
as if she had
just blown a peasant
and didn't like the taste

*

[...]

De sperma entossecata[91]
quella strea[92]
me futtea ...!

[...]

91 Entossecata: 'fatta', 'drogata'.
92 Strea: 'strega'.

*

Made of sperm
that witch
really fucked me over!

*

[...]

Ah quillo vagito anchora
de amante criatura
e' na buia cammora[93]
mannanno[94] fora
quill'uitimo[95] muto sospire

[...]

---

93 Cammora: 'camera'.
94 Mannanno: 'mandando'.
95 Uitimo: 'ultimo'.

*

Ah again that cry
Some creature making love
in some dark room
lets out again
that last dumb sigh

*

[...]

E quillo pure
que amava[96] piue
de onne animale
empeciati core a core

[...]

96   Amava: 'amavo'.

*

And that one too
I loved more
than any animal
stuck heart to heart

*

[…]

Que fo[97] quella vestia[98]
qu'aio audito de nocte
una donna feruta
o un pavone
saiettato en volo?

[…]

97   Fo: 'fu'.
98   Vestia: 'bestia'.

*

What was that beast
I heard crying in the night
A wounded woman
    or a peacock
    shot in flight?

*

[...]

O onne[99] omo
adormiverame teco[100]
frate[101] amatore
per meo bisuogno maggio[102]
ne la mea stremitate
adormiverame teco
per meo bisuogno maggio
et sugeravete
alataravete
bellecçe toa[103] como bella fiera[104].

[...]

99 Onne: 'ogni'.
100 Adormiverame teco: 'mi addormenterei con te'.
101 Frate: 'fratello'.
102 Maggio: 'maggiore'.
103 Bellecçe toa: 'la tua bellezza'.
104 Fiera: 'animale'.

*

Everyman
I'd sleep with thee
brother love
in my most need
in my extremity
sleep with thee
in my most need
and suck thee
suckle thee
o brute beauty

*

[...]

Dereto la banca[105] de la taberna
donne lo nome oblivisci mallem[106]
rem[107] fei na voita[108]
co la camairera de bus[to?][109]
per iscovrire ahi troppo tarde
lo sio secreto celare

[...]

---

105 La banca: 'il bancone'.
106 Oblivisci mallem (latino): 'preferirei dimenticare'.
107 Rem (latino): 'la cosa', cioè 'l'amplesso'.
108 Fein a voita: 'feci una volta'.
109 Bus[to?]: 'dal seno prorompente'.

*

Under the bar of a bodega
whose name I'd rather not remember
I once made it with the busty barmaid
Only to discover too late
her hidden secret . . .

*

[...]

Latroniuçça tosta[110] sotto lo ponne
la torrao[111] de scarçella[112]
forrata[113] de pelo [...]
ddiaceraola [...] gaudere[114]
et spiegharaola[115] [...]
pe'ffurare[116] l'aoro[117] que nce[118] [...]

[...]

110 Latroniuçça tosta: 'rapina, piccola ruberia'.
111 Torrao: 'prenderò'.
112 Scarçella: 'borsa'.
113 Forrata: 'foderata'.
114 Ddiaceraola gaudere: 'la metterò distesa per farla
     godere'.
115 Spiegharaola: 'la aprirò'.
116 Pe'ffurare: 'per rubare'.
117 L'aoro: 'l'oro'.
118 Nce: 'ci' (sottint. 'si trova').

[...]

A quick disguise
under the bridge
And I'll snatch her purse
the one with fur
I'll lay it down
and make it purr
and open it
and get the gold inside her

[...]

[...]

Berçato fora[119] n'aitro filglio de Roma
sopre li lencioli[120] a l'alba
vita prima que fatta desfatta
essare[121] potera[122] eroe del so[123] tiempo[124]
melglio ca d'esto
tepido empiasto[125]
de laite et de brina

[...]

119 Berçato fora: 'versato fuori'.
120 Lencioli: 'lenzuola'.
121 Essare: 'essere'.
122 Potera: 'avrebbe potuto'.
123 So: 'suo'.
124 Tiempo: 'tempo'.
125 Empiasto: 'impiastro'.

*

Spilled out another Roman son
upon the sheets at dawn
What a waste of life undone!
Could have been a hero in his time
Better than this
warm puddle
made of milk and brine

*

[…]

Nigra anema mea
per siempre
buco de merda
aio ventuto el nerbo[126] meo
a la puta

[…]

Sole vasso cielo mortu
manno nu iemito
vestia muta no mazarrata[127]
jemenne[128] a lo sole

[…]

126 Nerbo: 'membro virile'.
127 Mazarrata: 'battuta', 'massacrata'.
128 Jemenne: 'gemente'.

*

Black my soul
forevermore
whole hole of *merda*
Sold my cock
to a whore

*

Sun down Dead sky
I let out a cry
Dumb beast undone
wailing at the sun

*

[...]

Tristo vastardo[129] et veone
rebellante futtuto
[...] et tutto
sancto stollatore[130] de ienti
[...] mea vocca de veritate
o Sancta Maria Commedena
vocca de veritate
de moite faizitate[131]

[...]

129 Vastardo: 'bastardo'.
130 Stollatore: 'agitatore'.
131 De moite faizitate: 'di molte falsità'.

*

Drunken cocksman
two‑time bastard
rebel fucker
(anything in sight)
rabble‑rouser saint . . .
my Mouth of Truth
(o Santa Maria in Cosmedin)
full of the truth . . .
of many falsehoods

*

[...]

Vino vino ne le mee vene vino
cotica muscia[132] de vino
vino benedecto et vino dimoniecto
dimonio et sacramento
male dici [...]
et embracceca [...]
mare en me de sanguine
ebbro sucido vino

[...]

---

132 Cotica muscia: 'pelle flaccida'.

*

Vino vino vino in my veins
flabby body wineskin
Blessed vino devil vino
demon sacrament!
curse it
and embrace it
bloody sea in me
Drunken dirty wino . . .

*

[...]

Manu turbato[133]
cum manu plena[134] de argiglia[135] humida
en vasso[136] [...]
ah cad[ere] via [...]

[...]

133 Manu turbato (latino): 'masturbato'.
134 Cum manu plena (latino): 'con la mano piena'.
135 Argiglia: 'argilla'.
136 Vasso: 'basso'.

*

Jerked off

Hand full of wet clay

I lie back

Ah fall away

*

[…]

Ah ma lo sole vastardo[137]
anchora levase al maitino
como la vita mea
co lo nerbo ritto

[…]

137   Vastardo: 'bastardo'.

*

Ah but
bastard sun
still gets up in the morning
like my life
with a hard⁄on

*

[...]

Capo de caballo[138] ne lo lietto[139]
songno pauroso de caballa[140]
[...] no chabalca[141]
per la morta mea vita

[...]

138 Caballo: 'cavallo'.
139 Lietto: 'letto'.
140 Caballa: 'cavalla'.
141 Chabalca: 'cavalca'.

*

Horse's head in the bed
night
mare
rides no more
through my life dead

*

[...]

Aò Aò Aò
se n'va lo granne[142] destriero bicio[143]
callo pe'lla soa poletra[144]
como lo verro pe'lla scrofa

[...]

142 Granne: 'grande'.
143 Bicio: 'bigio'.
144 Poletra: 'puledra'.

*

Haw haw haw
goes the great grey stud
hot for his filly
like a boar for a whore

*

[...]

Ciciliani ferranti[145] [...]
merchati[146] pe'lle sangolenne[147] vattaglie[148]
frati animali muorti[149] menanno[150]
a lo maciello [...]
mentre que vaco[151] cacanno[152]

[...]

145 Ferranti: 'cavalli da tiro'.
146 Merchati: 'assoldati'.
147 Sangolenne: 'sanguinolente'.
148 Vattaglie: 'battaglie'.
149 Muorti: 'morti'.
150 Menanno: 'sospingendo'.
151 Vaco: 'vanno'.
152 Cacanno: 'cacando'.

*

Sicilian dray-horses
commandeered in bloody battles
now pull dead brother animals
to slaughterhouses
shitting as they go

*

[...]

Tre poletre e'n' largura[153] de rora[154]
guatano gire[155] le charrette de le vestie
odoranno[156] l'aere sangolenne
li occhi abafati
et li soccoli[157] de pece deventati

[...]

153 Largura: 'spizzato'.
154 Rore: 'rugiada'.
155 Gire: 'andare'.
156 Odoranno: 'odorando'.
157 Soccoli: 'zoccoli'.

*

Three free fillies in a field of dew
watch the animal hearses pass
smelling the bloody air
their eyes aglare
hooves turned to glue

*

[...]

Ne la taberna de la Banniera Nigra
s'ar[rebal]taro li schacchi [...]
et così vençe[158] [...]
[...] rege che chastello
chabaliero[159] e reina[160]
li baroni caddono cum pavura[161]
'nanti[162] la mea spada
tutti li fanni[163] co li nerbi ritti

[...]

---

158 Vençe: 'vinse'.
159 Chabaliero: 'cavalieri'.
160 Reina: 'regina'.
161 Cum pavura: 'con paura'.
162 'Nanti: 'davanti'.
163 Fanni: 'fanti'.

*

In the Black Flag Tavern
knocked the chess game over
and so o'ercame
both king and castle
knight and queen
Bishops fell with fear
before my spear
Foot soldier pawn with a hard⁄on

*

[...]

Citade faita[164] de romane ruine
[c]a salamora[165]!

[...]

Ceche et rupte[166] le estatue
ruite[167] ne l'herba
miranci suso
sospeccianne[168]
co li occhi votati
rite le vraccie[169] rotte
aue atque uale[170] !

[...]

164 Faita: 'fatta'.
165 [C]a salamora: 'che salamoia', ossia 'che casino'.
166 Rupte: 'rotte'.
167 Ruite: 'cadute'.
168 Sospeccianne: 'guardandoci con insistenza e timore'.
169 Vraccie: 'braccia'.
170 Aue atque uale: 'addio' (è la nota formula latina di
     salute).

*

City made of Roman ruins . . .
what a whorehouse!

*

The blind broken statues
tumbled among the grasses
stare up at us
stare out at us
with their empty eyes
their broken arms upraised
Hail + Farewell!

*

[...]

Sopre lo ponne Soblicio
Matta le iente mena
Na tuor[ma] de vestiame[171]
Su le soe zanche[172] dereto
Ululanno et guaienno[173]
[...] et movono banniere[174]
abrusciate de paraule[175]

[...]

171 Vestiame: 'bestiame'.
172 Zanche: 'zampe'.
173 Ululanno et guaienno: 'ululando e mugolando'.
174 Banniere: 'bandiere'.
175 Paraule: 'parole'.

*

Over Sublicio Bridge
the mob runs amok
a horde of beasts
on their hind legs
yowling and yammering
Except they're waving banners
burnt with words

*

[…]

Amare siempre te, patremo[176], pozzo[177]?
    prope Pyramide te lassaro
        como a despietto
      de lo nomato emperatoro
    te menerao finente a cca'[178]
      poscia tutto quillo dolore
        iacerai 'nanti de l'aitri
          fiero como simper

[…]

176 Patremo: 'patre mio'.
177 Pozzo: 'posso'.
178 Finente a 'cca: 'fino a casa'.

*

Father may I love you still?
By the Pyramid they left you
as a kind of affront
to the so-called
Emperor
I'll take you home again
Past all pain
You'll lie there
beyond them all
fierce as ever

*

[...]

Lassa ca me vengnono a prennere[179]
reialemenne[180] parati et vestuti
li lassarao habere [...]
li ricchi vastardi
co' la 'ncarnata mea bombarda
affocaoraoli

[...]

179 Prennere: 'prendere'.
180 Reialmenne: 'regalmente'.

*

Let them come and get me
in their royal robes
I'll let them have it
the rich bastards
With my flesh fire-hose
drown them!

*

89

[...]

Sancto Sebastiano pe'mme abrusciao[181]
lo lapidaro o l'apesao[182]
l'abruciaro ca staieve en pede
i' pe'lloro non abruscerao
né lo sio flumine transducerao[183]

[...]

<hr />

181 Abrusciao: 'bruciò'.
182 L'apesao: 'l'impiccarono'.
183 Transducerao: 'attraverserò'.

*

St. Sebastian burned for me
They stoned him
or hung him
burned him standing
But I'll not burn for them
I'll not cross *their* river . . .

*

[...]

Sanguine et margarite[184] sfatte
engromaco[185] li rote de le carrette
i' camminarao envece [...] a
caliditate de lo meo destino
've nulla[186] banniera
maie ne vene amainata

[...]

184 Margarite: 'perle'.
185 Engromaco: 'incrostano'.
186 Nulla: 'nessuna'.

*

Blood and broken pearls
clot their tumbril wheels
I'll walk instead
to my own hot fate
where no flag furls

*

[...]

Bagattino[187] pe'lla strada
de Cesare effigiato
mirame scaiçato[188]
et tutto varvato[189]
i' quillo ca t'ave conquistato!

[...]

---

187 Bagattino: 'moneta di poco valore'.
188 Scaiçato: 'scalzo'.
189 Varvato: 'barbuto'.

*

Coin on the cobblestone
head of Caesar
gapes at me
shoeless
unshaven
his conqueror!

— finis —

Originally published
by City Lights Italia, Firenze, 1997
© Lawrence Ferlinghetti

Manufactured in the United States of America
New Directions Books are printed on acid-free paper
First published as a New Directions Book in 2015
Design by Erik Rieselbach

Library of Congress Cataloging in Publication Data
Chiera, Lorenzo, 1348-1400.
[Poems. Selections. English]
Shards : fragments of verses / Lorenzo Chiera ; translation by
Lawrence Ferlinghetti with Massimiliano Chiamenti.
pages cm
ISBN 978-0-8112-2475-8 (alk. paper)
I. Ferlinghetti, Lawrence, translator.
II. Chiamenti, Massimiliano, translator. III. Title.
PQ4299.C35A2 2015
851'.2—dc23   2015022079

1 3 5 7 9 8 6 4 2

New Directions Books are published for James Laughlin
by New Directions Publishing Corporation
80 Eighth Avenue, New York 10011